MICROHABITATS

Life in a
CAVE

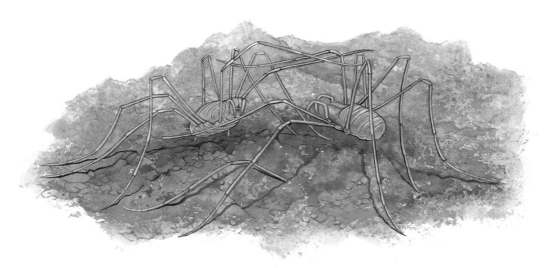

Clare Oliver

RAINTREE
STECK-VAUGHN
PUBLISHERS

A Harcourt Company

Austin   New York
www.raintreesteckvaughn.com

Published by Raintree Steck-Vaughn Publishers, an imprint of Steck-Vaughn Company.

Project Editors: Sean Dolan and Tamsin Osler
Production Manager: Richard Johnson
Illustrated by Stuart Lafford, Colin Newman, Dick Twinney
Designed by Ian Winton

Planned and produced by Discovery Books

Library of Congress Cataloging-in-Publication Data

Oliver, Clare.
Life in a cave/Clare Oliver.
p.cm. -- (Microhabitats)
Includes bibliographical references (p.).
ISBN 0-7398-4330-3
1. Cave animals--Juvenile literature. [1. Cave animals.] I. Title.

QL117 .044 2001
591.56'4--dc21

2001031677

Printed and bound in the United States
1 2 3 4 5 6 7 8 9 LB 07 06 05 04 03 02

Acknowledgments
The publishers would like to thank the following for permission to reproduce their pictures:
Front Cover: E. & D. Hosking/FLPA; p.7: Haroldo Palo, Jr./NHPA; p.8: David Hosking/FLPA;
p.9: Mark Jones/Oxford Scientific Films; p.10: David M. Dennis/Oxford Scientific Films; p.11: Max Gibbs/Oxford
Scientific Films; p.12: Joe McDonald/Bruce Coleman; p.15: Michael Tweedie/NHPA; p.16: L. Lee Rue/FLPA; p.17: Daniel
Heuclin/NHPA; p.20: E. & D. Hosking/FLPA; p.21: J.A.L. Cooke/Oxford Scientific Films; p.22: E. & D. Hosking/FLPA;
p.24: Stephen Dalton/NHPA; p.25: Mantis Wildlife Films/Oxford Scientific Films; p.26: Terry Whittaker/FLPA;
p.27: Fritz Polking/FLPA; p.28: Mark Newman/FLPA; p.29: Jargon & Christine Sohns/FLPA.

Contents

The Underground World

The Cave

Caves are self-contained worlds, or **microhabitats**. The main types of caves are limestone caves, sea caves, ice caves, and lava caves. Caves are cool, dark, and often damp. These conditions do not suit every living thing, but some forms of life do thrive there. Plants cannot survive without sunlight, although mosses and ferns may grow in the shady entrance to the cave. Bacteria and fungi, however, can survive away from the light. They live on bat **guano** (dung) or rotting leaves that blow into the cave.

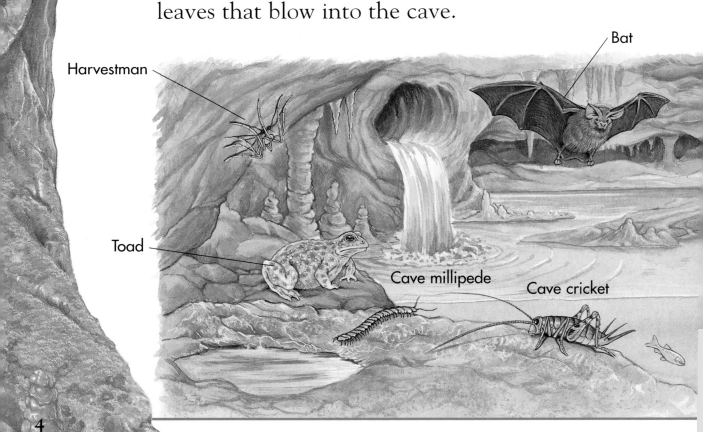

Harvestman

Bat

Toad

Cave millipede

Cave cricket

The cave provides many creatures a safe, quiet hiding place from **predators**. It offers protection from the weather and a consistent temperature throughout the year. Some creatures are so well-adapted to life in a cave that they never go outside. They are called **troglodytes**, from the Greek words meaning "in a cave."

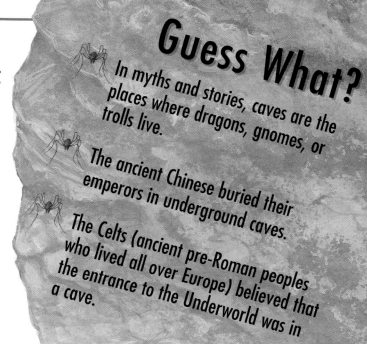

Guess What?

In myths and stories, caves are the places where dragons, gnomes, or trolls live.

The ancient Chinese buried their emperors in underground caves.

The Celts (ancient pre-Roman peoples who lived all over Europe) believed that the entrance to the Underworld was in a cave.

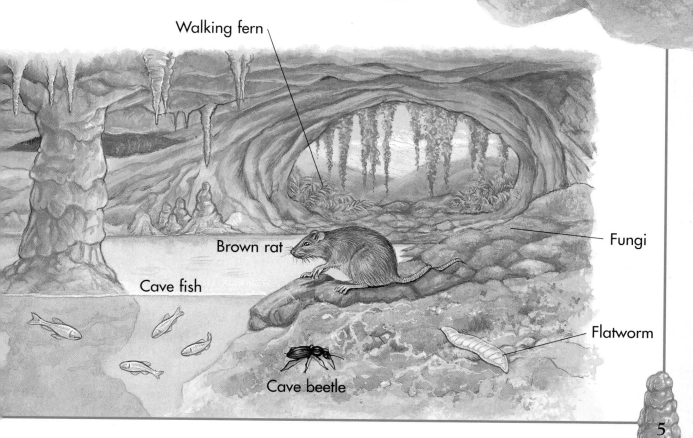

Walking fern

Fungi

Brown rat

Cave fish

Flatworm

Cave beetle

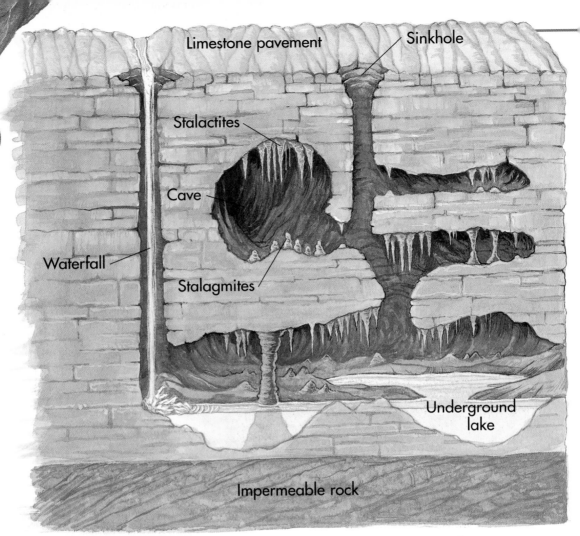

The most common type of cave is one that has formed in limestone rock (above). Often, it is part of a whole system of caves linked by tunnels.

Drips and Drops

Limestone rock is hard but it is also **soluble**. Over thousands of years, **acidic** surface water carves away at weak lines in the rock, dissolving it to form channels, hollows, and caves.

Caves often contain pillars made out of salt-like crystals. They are what is left behind when dripping water in the cave evaporates (turns into gas or vapor).

Columns that hang down from the roof of the cave are called **stalactites**. Columns that grow up from the cave floor are called **stalagmites**.

See for Yourself

Take two plastic cups and fill them with water. Stir in lots of Epsom salts — as much as you can make dissolve in the water. Dip a length of string in the water then stretch it out between the two cups with a saucer below the place where the string sags. Be patient! After four or five days, you will have your own stalactites and stalagmites.

All Sorts of Caves

Limestone caves are only one type of cave. Sea caves form along the seashore where waves and stones wear away holes in a cliff. Waves can even make a hole in the roof of a sea cave. This is called a blowhole, and water squirts out of it as the waves rush into the cave at high tide.

A group of California sea lions take shelter in a sea-washed cave.

Sea caves fill with the swirling tide twice a day, so few creatures are able to live there all the time. Only a few, tight-gripping barnacles are able to cling to the slippery rock without being washed out to sea. Seaweed, shellfish, and fish may be swept into the cave and left stranded between tides.

Cold Caves

In the Arctic and Antarctic, ice caves form where ice floes and icebergs are melted by warm sea currents. These caves sometimes provide shelter for penguins or seals. Scientists have also learned that there are even some microscopic life forms such as fungi and algae that can survive in the freezing conditions.

Emperor penguins, unique to Antarctica, have gathered near an ice cave formed by a grounded iceberg.

Slippery Swimmers

Underground Rivers

Rivers and streams flow along dark tunnels deep inside a cave system. The creatures that live in this water range from small flatworms and water snails to newts, crayfish, and fish. These animals make a **food chain**, with the smallest creatures surviving off rotting plant or animal matter in the water and then serving as food for larger predators.

The blind crayfish, like many cave-dwelling animals, is much paler than crayfish elsewhere.

Eyeless Wonders

Creatures that live deep in the cave are usually pale and blind. They do not need sight because they live in total darkness. Instead, they use other senses. Cave fish (below) have touch organs all over their body that enable them to "feel" their way.

Guess What?

The blind cave newt is pinkish-white, but it turns black if it is carried out into the sunlight.

Cave salamanders ooze a sticky substance from their skin. This allows them to walk up cave walls.

In 1999, scientists discovered a new type of eyeless crayfish in caves in Missouri.

In and Out

Salamanders, like frogs and toads, are amphibians. In their adult form, they can move between the water and the cave floor, as long as they keep their slimy body moist. Some salamanders never leave the cave. Others, like the cave salamander, will live anywhere—so long as it is dark, damp, and cavelike.

Creepy-Crawlies

Eight-Legged Monsters

The spiders that live in caves are hunters that chase prey rather than trap it in webs. Cave spiders include wolf spiders and cellar spiders.

Wolf spiders have good eyesight and can move very quickly in pursuit of insects and other prey.

Sting in the Tail

In caves in the United States and many other parts of the world, you may find scorpions. These night hunters thrive in the dark of the cave. They use the sting at the end of their tail to stun prey such as spiders and insects.

Whip spiders and whip scorpions also live in the cave. Both creatures have flattened bodies and can slide into cracks to avoid predators.

Spider-like harvestmen lurk at the cave mouth, where they catch huge numbers of flies. They have very long legs with a tiny claw at their tip.

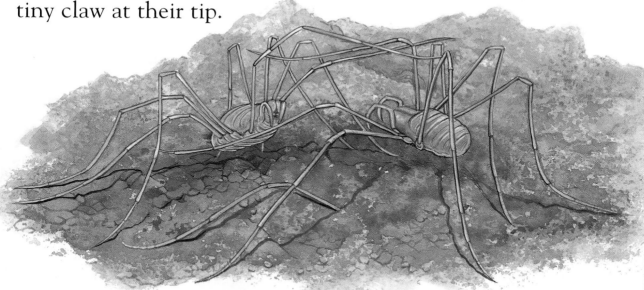

A male harvestman, or daddy longlegs, may bite off a leg of his opponent as they fight over a female.

See for Yourself

This is what a spider's egg sac looks like. Many arachnids, including wolf spiders and whip scorpions, carry their egg sacs to prevent them from being eaten.

Next time you see a wolf spider, count how many eyes it has. The large ones are easy to spot, but what about the four smaller eyes?

Lots of Legs

Also found scurrying around in the dark of the cave are unusual minibeasts known as myriapods, which means "many-footed animals." There are two basic types: centipedes and millipedes. Both have huge numbers of legs and feet, but apart from that they are quite different.

Fast Runners

Centipedes are fast-moving hunters. The most likely type to be found in a cave are scutigerids—short centipedes with 15 pairs of very long legs.

Like all centipedes, scutigerids use their claws, which lie just below their mouth, to inject poison into their prey.

When threatened, pill millipedes curl up into a ball.

Eating Leftovers

Each time a millipede sheds its skin, it grows more segments—and more legs! Millipedes are slow-moving vegetarians. Although no plants grow in the cave, they find plenty to eat. The wind blows in leaves, bats drop seeds, and millipedes even find bat guano tasty.

Millipede means "1,000 legs," but none have more than 750.

See for Yourself

Take a close look at a centipede. It has a pair of legs on each segment of its body.

Now, use a lens to look at a millipede. Millipedes have two pairs of legs on each of their body segments. Some millipedes have as many as 190 segments, others may have only 13.

Crickets, Crawlers, and Beetles

Cave-dwelling insects include crickets (below), rock crawlers, and beetles. Although cave crickets sleep inside the cave, each night they leave to feed on the plants that grow at the cave mouth and beyond. Their long antennae or feelers help them to sense predators in the dark, since these crickets are an important source of food for larger animals.

Dead Meat

Rock crawlers look a bit like earwigs, with very small eyes or even none at all. Because they do not rely on sight, it does not matter to them whether it is night or day—they hunt around the clock. Rock crawlers are **scavengers** that look for dead creatures to eat. They also eat slow-moving prey.

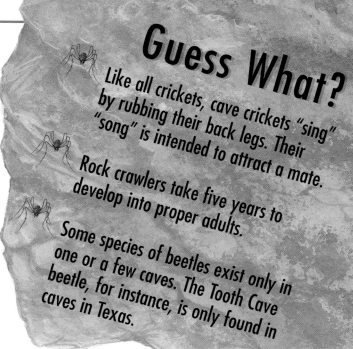

Different types of beetles may visit caves, but only some live there exclusively. Cave-dwelling beetles (left) are often eyeless and depend on a sharp sense of smell to find food. Some eyeless cave beetles feed solely on cricket eggs and their **larvae**.

Mites and Parasites

Bat guano is a rich food for many different life forms. Blind springtails, bristletails, and silverfish eat their way through the rotting dung. Adapted to life in a cave, these primitive small, wingless insects have soft, pale bodies. They are also found on fungus and other **organic** matter in the cave.

The springtail is named for its tail. When not in use, its tail is folded under its abdomen. By flicking it downwards, the insect is catapulted through the air.

Freeloaders

In the cave, as in all habitats, all creatures live off other living things in some way. However, fleas, mites, and ticks are true parasites because they feed on others without killing them. Bat fleas drink the blood of bats, for example.

Bat flies, or bat bugs (below), are among the most unusual of these creatures. Despite their name, adult bat flies have no wings. The female bat fly keeps her eggs inside her body—as well as the young larvae when they hatch.

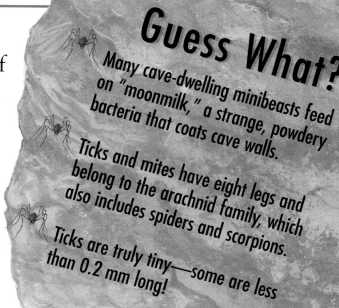

Guess What?

Many cave-dwelling minibeasts feed on "moonmilk," a strange, powdery bacteria that coats cave walls.

Ticks and mites have eight legs and belong to the arachnid family, which also includes spiders and scorpions.

Ticks are truly tiny—some are less than 0.2 mm long!

As the larva develops, it turns into a **pupa**, a sort of sleeping state, and the mother bat fly lays the pupa on the wall of the bat roost. An adult bat fly only comes out from this pupa state when it senses a bat nearby. It climbs onto the bat host and takes its first drink of blood!

Tiny Ticks

A tick usually measures less than .05 inch (1mm) long but swells up greatly after feeding.

After feeding

Before feeding

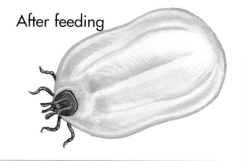

A Place to Sleep

Roosting Bats

Bats are probably the best-known cave dwellers. During the daytime, cool, damp caves are an ideal place for roosting bats.

Some bats are solitary, which means that they live alone. Others nest together in enormous colonies. Some bats live in the cave throughout the year, while others go there for a single season, either to nest or **hibernate**. Different types of bats may even roost in the same cave.

A horseshoe bat hibernates by hanging upside down from a rock. Both the greater and the lesser horseshoe bat like to live in caves.

Batty Effects

The presence of large bat colonies in a cave can alter the microhabitat. Their body heat can raise the cave temperature to about 100° Fahrenheit (38° Celsius). Bats breathe in oxygen and breathe out carbon dioxide. The level of carbon dioxide, together with ammonia (a poisonous gas produced by the bat guano) reduces the amount of oxygen in the cave. This makes for a natural limit to the number of bats and other mammals that can live there.

As dusk falls, bats wake from their daytime roost and prepare to leave the cave in search of food.

Guess What?

Thirteen species of bats are considered endangered. Nine of these species are found in the United States.

The Alabama cave fish survives in just one cave, under one bat roost. If that bat colony were lost, the cave fish would become extinct.

Bats on the Hunt

Bats are nocturnal animals. They have a highly developed method for pinpointing their insect prey. It's called **echolocation**. Although not **audible** to humans, as they fly through the air, bats make short, high-pitched squeaks. When their squeaks hit objects, such as moths, these sounds bounce back to the bats as echoes. From these echoes, bats can navigate and find prey in the dark.

The horseshoe bat preys on flies, beetles, spiders, and moths.

Finding a Meal

1. The bat sends out slow high-pitched squeaks that travel as sound waves.

2. The squeaks bounce back off a moth as an echo.

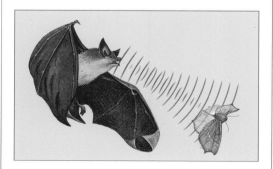

3. From the echo, the bat can pinpoint where the moth is.

Guess What?

The Chinese consider bats to be a sign of good luck. The Chinese word Fu means both "bat" and "happiness."

Blood-sucking vampire bats really do exist in South America. They feed on the blood of larger animals, especially cattle. Human vampires exist only in stories.

The noises bats make that humans can hear are not for echolocation. These noises are how bats communicate with each other.

Mothy Meals

Because it takes a lot of energy to fly, bats eat almost constantly when they are awake. In one night, a large colony of free-tailed bats can eat 100 tons of insects! Moths are common prey, mainly because they are night-fliers, too. In tropical regions, there are **species** of bat that feed on fruit, frogs, or even fish.

Bat Nurseries

Sometimes, bats fly to a particular cave to give birth. Each year, for example, around 10 million Mexican free-tailed bats travel more than 750 miles (1,200 km) to reach Bracken Cave, Texas. Each one gives birth to a single baby.

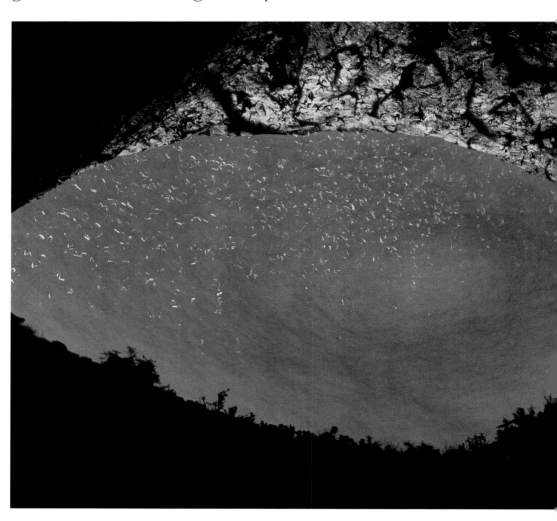

The Bat Cave in Carlsbad Caverns, New Mexico, is well-named. Each summer millions of bats roost there.

Hide and Seek

Bat mothers cannot carry their young with them when they go out hunting. Instead, they leave their young behind and fly back throughout the night to feed them milk. There may be millions of young bats in a "nursery," but a mother finds her own offspring easily—even if it has moved from where she left it. It seems she can recognize its call and its scent!

Bats are mammals, which means they give birth to live young that feed on their mother's milk.

Cave Visitors

Bats are not the only mammals that seek shelter in a cave. Other mammal visitors include mice, rats, wildcats, raccoons, and wolves. In the United States, brown and black bears (below) shelter in caves, especially during the winter months when they live off the fat they have stored in their bodies. Unlike mice or other animals, bears do not truly hibernate. They wake from time to time to eat, and their heart rate and breathing does not slow down as in other hibernating animals.

Sneaky Predators

Birds and reptiles will venture into the mouth of a cave to escape the winter winds. Vultures, owls, and snakes are also tempted by the hope of a meal—perhaps of a young bat!

Guess What?

Many thousands of years ago, people sometimes lived in caves, too. They left behind some of the earliest known works of art. Cave wall paintings of animals at Lascaux, in France, are 20,000 years old.

Caves in Missouri contain the remains of prehistoric animals, including saber-toothed tigers.

Some creatures become accidental visitors to caves, falling in through a hole in the ground above the cave.

All of these visitors add to the cave microhabitat. Their dung, fur, or feathers will provide food or shelter for minibeasts and other small creatures.

Barn owls may feed on snails, as well as on mice, frogs, and voles.

Caves Around the World

Amazing Cave Dwellers

Caves are found all over the world. Their inhabitants differ from region to region. Sometimes, animals are unique to one particular cave. Endangered eyeless catfish are found only in a handful of Mexican caves, for example.

Tropical rain forest caves provide a home to a rich and diverse array of animal life including some unusual birds and bats.

Flying High

Some of the most unusual cave dwellers are birds that use echolocation in the same way that bats do. Oilbirds (above), which live in tropical regions of South and Central America, use echolocation, and so do the cave swifts (or swiftlets) of Asia and Australia. Flying foxes and other fruit bats also live in tropical caves. These bats rely more on sight than echolocation to find their sugary foods of fruit or flowers full of nectar. Their guano provides food for cave-dwelling cockroaches.

Guess What?

The larvae of fungus gnats, which live in caves in New Zealand and Australia, glow in the dark. They use sticky threads hung from the rocks to trap flying insects!

The saliva or spit produced by a cave swift to cement its nest is considered a delicacy (a rare and tasty food) by some people. They risk their lives to collect the nests, from which they make birds' nest soup.

Glossary

Acidic (AS-sid-ik) Containing a high level of acid.

Arachnids (ARAK-nidz) A group of arthropods, or invertebrates, that have eight jointed legs. Arachnids include spiders, scorpions, ticks, and mites.

Audible (AW-duh-buhl) A sound that is loud enough to be heard.

Echolocation (EK-oh-loh-KAY-shuhn) Using the echoes of sound waves to navigate and find prey.

Food chain Links between plants and animals in a microhabitat that reflects the way energy, in the form of food, passes from one species of organism to another.

Guano (gwah-NOH) The excrement of bats or seabirds.

Hibernate (HYE-bur-nay-shuhn) A very deep sleep that helps some animals to survive the winter.

Impermeable (im-PUR-mee-uh-buhl) A material that does not allow fluids to pass through it.

Larvae (LAR-vee) The immature form of an insect before it becomes an adult.

Microhabitat (MYE-kroh-HAB-uh-tat) A small, specialized place, such as a tide pool or freshwater pond, where particular animals and plants live and grow.

Organic (or-GAN-ik) Plant or animal matter.

Predator (PRED-uh-tur) An animal that hunts other animals for food.

Pupa (PYOO-puh) The stage in an insect's life when the larva changes into an adult.

Scavenger (SKAV-uhn-jur) An animal or organism that eats or otherwise uses waste materials, such as decaying animal bodies or guano.

Soluble (SOL-yuh-buhl) Able to be dissolved, like sugar dissolves in coffee.

Species (SPEE-sheez or SPEE-seez) A specific type of animal or plant.

Stalactites (stu-LAK-titez) Rock formations that hang down from the ceiling of a cave. They occur in places where limestone-rich water that has seeped out of the rock collects and drips to the cave floor.

Stalagmites (stuh-LAG-mitez) Rock formations that grow up in column form from the floor of a cave. Stalagmites form where water drips down from the ceiling of the cave.

Troglodyte (truh-gla-DITE) A cave dweller.

Further Reading

Bevan, Finn. *Beneath the Earth: The Facts and The Fables*. Danbury, CT: Children's Press, 1999.

Gallant, Roy A. *Limestone Caves*. Danbury, CT: Franklin Watts, Incorporated, 1998.

Morris, Neil. *Caves*. New York: Crabtree Publishing, 1995.

Schulz, Ronald. *Looking Inside Caves and Caverns* (X-Ray Vision). Emeryville, CA: Avalon Travel Publishing, 1993.

Index